bake me I'm yours...

chocolate

Tracey Mann

D&C
David and Charles

For my husband Chris and my two beautiful girls, Charlotte and Kelly

A DAVID & CHARLES BOOK
Copyright © David & Charles Limited 2009, 2010

David & Charles is an F+W Media Inc. company,
4700 East Galbraith Road
Cincinnati, OH 45236

First published in 2009
This paperback edition first published in the UK
in 2010
Reprinted 2010 (twice)

Text and designs copyright © Tracey Mann
2009, 2010
Photography copyright © David & Charles
2009, 2010

Names of manufacturers, ingredients and other
products are provided for the information of
readers, with no intention to infringe copyright or
trademarks.

A catalogue record for this book is available from
the British Library.

ISBN-13: 978-0-7153-3764-6 paperback
ISBN-10: 0-7153-3764-5 paperback

Printed in China by Toppan Leefung
Printing Limited
for David & Charles
Brunel House   Newton Abbot   Devon

Commissioning Editor: Jennifer Fox-Proverbs
Editor: Emily Rae
Project Editor: Bethany Dymond
Designer: Mia Farrant
Production Controllers: Kelly Smith
Photographer: Simon Whitmore

David & Charles publish high quality books on
a wide range of subjects.
For more great book ideas visit: **www.rucraft.co.uk**

contents

chocolate heaven...

Chocolate instantly conjures up a variety of images, whether it's hunting for chocolate eggs at Easter, giving a box of truffles to your sweetheart on Valentine's Day or simply indulging with chocolate fondue at a girls' night in.

As a self-taught cake decorator, my interest in decorating with chocolate began eight years ago with an increasing demand from brides for chocolate wedding cakes. Through my usual route of trial and error I have enjoyed designing some spectacular creations in chocolate over the years, and I now hope that I can share my creative insights into chocolate design with you.

In the front section (pp. 8–37), you will find a range of tasty recipes for cakes, brownies, bites and truffles. Discover all the essential techniques, including how to temper chocolate, use chocolate paste and achieve fabulous results with moulds.

When it comes to decorating with chocolate, the possibilities are endless. Experiment with a myriad of patterns and colours using transfer sheets to bring a whole new dimension to your creations and learn to create a range of beautiful, realistic flowers from chocolate paste, including three of my favourites: roses, orchids and gerberas.

The chocolate creations are divided up into five irresistible sections. Fall in love with chocolate with True Love (pp. 38–55) and explore a spectacular array of cakes and favours in Wedded Bliss (pp. 56–71). Get the party started with a fabulous range of Birthday Treats (pp. 72–87) and have a chocolaty Christmas with Festive Indulgence (pp. 88–103). For those of you who could celebrate every day with chocolate, take a look at the delicious treats in More Excuses (pp. 104–117).

My personal favourite design is the Born to be Wild birthday cake (see pp. 74–77), which really makes the most of a striking leopard print transfer sheet pattern to create a bold and contemporary, clean-lined statement; a design route I like to follow with all of my work. I also love the Sunny Delights cupcakes (pp. 82–83), which look so fresh and funky and inject my favourite colour into chocolate.

Whenever you want to create a chocolate masterpiece, even when you are short of time, you will find the perfect project here, from spectacular wedding cakes and breath-taking birthday cakes to small, quick-to-make truffles, cupcakes and lollipops. By following a few simple rules you can really impress your friends and family with your wonderful creations. The only limit is your imagination. Chocolate has never been so much fun!

Tracey

www.traceyscakes.co.uk

basics

Before you begin to bake with chocolate, it is worth familiarizing yourself
with the tools and equipment that you will need and getting to grips with key
skills such as tempering chocolate (pp. 10–11), working with chocolate paste
(pp. 12–13) and dowelling cakes (pp. 14–15) for impressive multi-tiered effects.

basic tool kit

The following is a list of equipment frequently used in the book, most of which can be found in good sugarcraft stores. In addition specific requirements are listed in the recipe 'you will needs' and supplier's abbreviated details follow in brackets where applicable. For details of suppliers, refer to pp. 118-119.

- **Dresden tool** ① for making markings on paste, used in conjunction with the sugar gun
- **Glue stick** for attaching ribbon to cake boards
- **Greaseproof paper** ② for lining cake tins
- **Icing sugar** ③ use when rolling out chocolate paste to prevent it sticking to the work surface
- **Kitchen roll** for wiping up any spillages
- **Knife** ④ sharp and non-serrated, for cutting out shapes
- **Paintbrush** ⑤ for dusting and painting
- **Piping bag, disposable** ⑥ for piping tempered chocolate

- **Plastic side scraper** ⑦ for trimming chocolate paste on cakes
- **Palette knife** ⑧ for spreading chocolate and applying buttercream
- **Rolling pin** ⑨ for rolling out chocolate paste
- **Scissors** ⑩ for cutting transfer sheets to size
- **Smoother** ⑪ for creating a smooth, even finish when covering cakes with chocolate paste
- **Tape measure** ⑫ to measure transfer sheets
- **Work board, non-stick** ⑬ used for rolling out chocolate paste

store them away

- Once you have made your chocolates or cakes, always store them in cool, dry, dark conditions – chocolate will melt very quickly if left in direct sunlight.
- Avoid refrigerating your chocolate as it will begin to gather condensation when returned to room temperature. Excessive moisture will cause 'sugar bloom', meaning that the sugar rises to the surface of the chocolate causing discolouration.
- Chocolate absorbs odours so do not store it near anything with a strong scent.

tempering chocolate

Chocolate contains cocoa butter crystals and tempering is a process of heating chocolate so that these crystals are uniform. Correctly tempered chocolate will produce an end result that is smooth-tasting, crisp, even-coloured and shiny, while incorrectly tempered chocolate produces a dull or streaky end result often referred to as a 'bloom', which while not inedible, does look unsightly and will taste grainy. Incorrectly tempered chocolate will not set very well, will 'bend' rather than 'snap', and will not release easily from moulds, so before placing chocolate into a mould ensure it is correctly tempered.

If you are mixing chocolate together with other ingredients such as cream in truffles, it will not need to be tempered

Tempered chocolate is useful for attaching edible embellishments, such as the coloured circles on the Easter Extravaganza cake (see pp. 106–109).

types of chocolate

There are two types of chocolate available: couverture chocolate and confectioner's coating chocolate, and all of the items in this book have been made using couverture chocolate. Couverture chocolate usually contains a minimum of 32 per cent cocoa butter and its taste is by far superior to coating chocolate, which can contain little or no cocoa butter. Couverture chocolate must go through the process of tempering prior to use in order to produce a shiny chocolate that 'snaps' when broken.

how to temper chocolate

The simplest method is to purchase chocolate couverture callets or buttons, which have already been through one of the processes of tempering. With extreme care, these can be melted in a small plastic bowl in the microwave in short 10 second bursts on full power (850w), mixing thoroughly between each interval. Alternatively, follow the steps below:

1 Melt the chocolate to 45°C (113°F) over a double boiler, being extremely careful not to allow any steam or water to come into contact with the chocolate. Once the chocolate is melted, remove from the heat.

2 Add approximately one-third again of couverture callets to the melted chocolate and stir until melted. This will begin to bring the temperature of

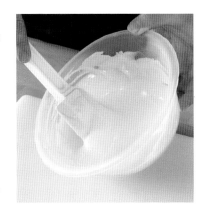

the chocolate down. Using a chocolate thermometer, dark chocolate should be cooled to 31°C (88°F), milk chocolate to 30°C (86°F), and white chocolate to 29°C (84°F).

3 Dip a clean palette knife into the chocolate to test it. Allow it to set for 2–3minutes. If it sets hard, snaps easily and has a shiny gloss, it is ready for use.

Many tempering machines are available to purchase (see Suppliers (k) and (hcf) on pp. 118–119)

chocolate paste

Chocolate paste is made up from Belgian chocolate, glucose and water. The glucose makes the chocolate pliable so that it can be rolled out and used to cover cakes, to mould flowers (see pp. 32–37) and to create decorations, such as on the Blossom Delights mini cakes (see pp. 66–67). Chocolate paste is available in white, milk and dark chocolate and strawberry, orange, lemon and cappuccino flavours, and it can be used with a variety of cake decorating equipment, such as moulds (see p. 26) and bead makers (see p. 25). It usually has a four to six month shelf life and is readily available from cake decorating stores (see Suppliers pp. 118–119).

chocolate paste vs. sugarpaste

There is a common confusion between chocolate paste and chocolate flavoured sugarpaste. However, chocolate paste is unlike sugarpaste, as it reacts to the heat of your hands – the more you knead it, the stickier it becomes as it starts to melt.

Chocolate paste must be rolled out on lots of icing sugar to prevent it sticking to the work surface. You may need to initially warm the product for a short time (about 5–10 seconds in a microwave) if the paste is particularly hard. If you have overheated the paste and it has become extremely sticky, place it in a polythene bag, and pop it in the fridge for an hour. The paste will start to harden again.

covering cakes with chocolate paste

To cover cakes with chocolate paste, follow these simple steps:

1 Apply a thin layer of buttercream to the cake to help the chocolate paste stick.

2 Roll out the paste to a depth of about 4mm (⁵⁄₃₂in). Lift the paste carefully over the top of the cake, supporting it with a rolling pin, and positioning the paste so that it covers the cake.

3 Smooth the surface of the cake using a smoother for the flat areas and a combination of the smoother and the palm of your hand for the curved areas.

4 Take the smoother and, while pressing down, run the flat edge around the base of the cake to create a cutting line. Trim away the excess paste with a palette knife.

Avoid working with chocolate paste in a hot environment as it melts very quickly

storing chocolate paste

⚜ Once you have covered your cake, store it in a box at room temperature, away from direct sunlight and strong odours.

⚜ Do not be tempted to store a covered cake in the fridge, otherwise it will gather condensation when it is removed from the chilled environment.

⚜ Put any excess paste in a tied food grade plastic bag and keep in cool, dry, dark conditions.

coloured cocoa butter

Coloured cocoa butter is purchased in bottles and comes in a range of shades, including pink, orange, green and black. The product is solid and requires heating before use. Place in a microwave, ensuring the lid is open and heat on full power (850w) for 30 seconds. Remove the bottle from the microwave, replace the lid and shake to mix. Repeat this process until fully melted.

dowelling cakes

To assemble a multi-tiered cake, you need to create an internal support system to prevent it from collapsing. Dowels are specially designed to prevent each tier from sinking into the one underneath. They can be made from plastic or wood, but must be food graded. To dowel a cake, carefully follow the steps below:

1 Measure the diameter of the cake you wish to place on top of the bottom tier. Cut out a piece of greaseproof paper matching the size of this smaller tier.

2 Place the greaseproof paper onto the surface of the lower cake as a guide. Gently indent the surface covered by the greaseproof paper with a dowelling rod to mark the position of each dowel. For maximum support, use at least five dowelling rods per cake plus one central rod.

3 Push one rod vertically down through the centre of the cake until it touches the cake board. Make a knife scratch or pencil mark on the dowel to mark its height in relation to the cake's surface.

4 Remove the dowel and, using a hacksaw or knife, cut on the marked line.

5 Cut a further five rods to exactly the same size, using the cut dowel as a measure.

6 Position all six rods into the cake as marked. Spread a layer of chocolate buttercream onto the cake surface then rest the top cake on the rods. Check the cake is level before proceeding to stack other layers on top.

To achieve an even level, it is very important that all the dowels are cut to the same size

recipes

Here you will find delicious tried-and-tested recipes for all of my chocolate creations, including chocolate sponge, cupcakes, bites, brownies and truffles.

chocolate sponge

This basic chocolate sponge cake recipe always goes down well. It is simply made with butter, caster sugar, eggs, cocoa powder and self-raising flour, and its size can easily be adapted using the quantity guide opposite.

	butter	caster sugar	eggs (medium)	cocoa powder	self-raising flour	cooking time
10cm (4in)	100g (3oz)	100g (3oz)	2	25g (1oz)	100g (3oz)	1 hour
15cm (6in)	175g (6oz)	175g (6oz)	3	25g (1oz)	175g (6oz)	1¼ hours
20cm (8in)	440g (14oz)	440g (14oz)	7	35g (1½oz)	440g (14oz)	1¾ hours
25cm (10in)	630g (22oz)	630g (22oz)	10	55g (2oz)	630g (22oz)	2–2½ hours

1 Pre-heat the oven to 160°C–170°C (325–338°F).

2 Line the sides and base of the cake tin with greaseproof paper.

3 Cream the butter and sugar together in a bowl.

4 Add the eggs one at a time with a tablespoon of self-raising flour.

5 Sieve the remaining flour and cocoa powder into the mixture and carefully fold it in with a metal spoon.

6 Spoon the mixture into the tin and bake in the centre of the oven, adjusting the cooking time according to the grid shown above.

7 Remove the cake from the oven and leave to cool in its tin for a few minutes before carefully placing onto a cooling rack.

Test if your cakes are cooked by inserting a skewer into the centre. If the skewer comes out clean, the cake is ready

cupcakes

These individual chocolate cupcakes make a wonderful indulgent treat and are perfect for weddings, tea parties or even just for lunch! Simply follow the instructions below:

ingredients (for 12 muffin-sized cupcakes) ...

- ❀ 225g (8oz) caster sugar
- ❀ 225g (8oz) butter
- ❀ 175g (6oz) self-raising flour
- ❀ 55g (2oz) cocoa powder
- ❀ 4 large eggs
- ❀ 1 tsp baking powder

For a treat, add 55g (2oz) of chocolate chips when you add the flour into the mixture

1 Pre-heat the oven to 180°C (350°F). Place the cases into a muffin bun tray.

2 Beat the sugar and butter together for a couple of minutes in a food processor. Alternatively, mix with a hand-held whisk.

3 Add one egg at a time with a tablespoon of flour.

4 Once all the eggs have been integrated, sieve the remaining flour, baking powder and cocoa powder and slowly incorporate into the mixture, either using a food mixer set to a slow pulse setting or folding in with a metal spoon.

5 Spoon the mixture into the cases, until they are about two-thirds full.

6 Bake in the oven for approximately 20 minutes or until the tops of the cakes spring back when lightly touched.

7 Allow the cupcakes to cool on wire racks.

brownies

These melt-in-the-mouth chocolate brownies are for the most serious of chocoholics only! They look wonderful when decorated with chocolate paste ribbons and presented in a gift box for a special occasion.

If desired, add 55g (2oz) of walnut pieces after beating, always remembering to first check if the recipient has a nut allergy

ingredients (for nine brownies) ...

- ❀ 175g (6oz) caster sugar
- ❀ 65g (2½oz) butter
- ❀ 65g (2½oz) self-raising flour
- ❀ 55g (2oz) Belgian dark chocolate buttons or grated chocolate
- ❀ 2 eggs
- ❀ 18cm (7in) square tin

1 Pre-heat the oven to 180°C (350°F). Grease and line the 18cm (7in) square tin.

2 Melt the butter and chocolate in a microwave at full power (850w) for approximately 20 seconds, or over a pan of hot water.

3 Stir in the caster sugar then sift the flour into a bowl and add to the mixture. Add the melted chocolate, sugar, butter and eggs to the mixture.

4 Beat the mixture until smooth and pour into the 18cm (7in) tin. Bake in the oven for approximately 35 minutes.

5 Remove from the oven, allow to cool, then cut into 6 x 6cm (2⅜ x 2⅜in) squares using a sharp knife.

chocolate bites

These mouth-watering chocolate bites are so simple to make and don't even require any baking. They can either be made as indulgent cookies for yourself or to give as gifts – simply use a variety of cookie cutters to vary the size of your bite.

ingredients (for nine small bites or four larger bites) ...

- ❀ 12 digestive biscuits (Graham crackers)
- ❀ 250g (9oz) white, milk or dark chocolate
- ❀ 55g (2oz) butter
- ❀ 60ml (4 tbsp) drinking chocolate
- ❀ 30ml (2 tbsp) golden syrup
- ❀ 18cm (7in) tin
- ❀ Round, metal cookie cutters

Do not let the chocolate set completely, or it will be difficult to cut out the individual bites

1 Melt the butter and golden syrup together in a pan over a low heat. Add the drinking chocolate.

2 Crush 12 digestive biscuits in a bag with a rolling pin. Add the melted mixture to the crushed biscuits. Push the mixture into the tin until it is flat and chill for approximately 20 minutes.

3 Temper 250g (9oz) of the chocolate of your choice, pour onto the mixture and spread into an even layer using a palette knife. Tap the tin to remove any air bubbles and leave for approximately 10 minutes at room temperature until the mixture is partially set.

4 Before the chocolate has gone completely hard use the round metal cutters to cut out the bites. Leave to harden before decorating as desired.

ganache

Ganache is a delicious variety of icing that can be used to fill chocolates, chocolate truffles and other desserts. It can be used as an alternative to chocolate buttercream to fill a cake, or can be poured over a cake that has already had a thin coating of chocolate paste.

ingredients (for one batch) ...

- 180ml (6fl oz) heavy cream
- 200g (7oz) dark chocolate
- 25g (1oz) butter

1 Heat the cream and the butter and pour over the chopped, dark chocolate.

2 Stir or blend the mixture until smooth. If desired, the mixture can be enhanced with liqueurs or extracts.

Be careful not to overheat the ganache or it may melt the chocolate cases

truffles

These delightful truffles are quick and simple to create, yet make a big impression as a wonderful alternative to shop-bought chocolates. If stored in cool, dark and dry conditions, they will keep for approximately a week.

Add 2 tsp of brandy or gin to the mixture to flavour your truffles and allow them to stay fresh for longer

ingredients
(for 15 truffles) ...

- 225g (8oz) dark chocolate
- 25g (1oz butter)
- 15ml (1 tbsp) single cream
- 2 egg yolks

1 Melt the chocolate and butter in a double boiler and add the egg yolks and single cream. Stir the mixture then allow to cool.

2 Roll the mixture into balls and dip them in dark tempered chocolate (see pp. 10–11).

chocolate buttercream

Chocolate buttercream can be used as a delicious filling between cake layers, as a topping for cupcakes and mini cakes, or simply as a base for attaching chocolate paste decorations or chocolate curls to your creations. It can be stored in a fridge for up to three weeks. Cover with cling film to prevent it from drying out.

ingredients (for one batch) ...

If the mixture becomes too stiff, simply add a little water

- 1kg (2lb 4oz) icing sugar
- 500g (1lb 2oz) butter
- 500g (1lb 2oz) Belgian chocolate

1 Cream the butter until its colour lightens.

2 Sift the icing sugar and thoroughly mix with the butter.

3 Melt the Belgian chocolate over a pan of hot water or in a microwave at full power (850w) for 20 second intervals, stirring between each time then heating again until fully melted. Add to the mix.

fabulous flavours

A few drops of oil will flavour buttercream without changing the consistency (see Suppliers (k), p.118).

Dark chocolate mint: add peppermint oil to a dark chocolate buttercream mix.
Milk chocolate orange: use milk chocolate and add orange oil to the mix.
White chocolate lemon: add lemon oil to a white chocolate and buttercream recipe.

decorations

Once you have mastered the basics and perfected your recipes, you can now go to town with the decoration to make your chocolate creations extra special. Here, you will discover how to use a sugar gun and beadmaker to achieve wonderful effects with moulds and to experiment with transfer sheets for impressive results.

sugar gun

The sugar gun is an extremely versatile tool when used with chocolate paste. By changing the nozzle attachments, the paste can be used to uniformly pipe a number of shapes, such as lines, ribbons and even a feather-like effect, as in the Easter Extravaganza chick (see pp. 106–109).

For best results, gently knead the chocolate paste until it is tacky before placing it into the gun. Squeeze the gun and use a Dresden tool to help remove the paste from it.

beadmaker

Using a beadmaker is a quick and easy way to create beautiful pearls of chocolate that are fantastic for decorating a wedding cake, such as White Wedding (see pp. 58–61). The chocolate paste beads can be dusted with a pearlized edible dust before use to create a beautiful sheen.

1 Sprinkle your board with icing sugar. Roll out a long strip of chocolate paste to the same length as the beadmaker. If the paste sticks to the mould, add more icing sugar.

2 Press the strip into the beadmaker then close it. Remove any excess paste on top with a plastic scraper.

3 Tip the beadmaker down so that it faces the work surface and carefully remove the 'beads' by gently pulling at the paste. Attach the strip of beads to your cake using a little tempered chocolate (see p. 11).

If you have 'hot hands', don't continually re-roll a piece of paste because it will become sticky, leave it to one side until cool

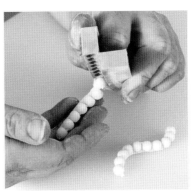

chocolate moulds

Using moulds is a quick and simple way of forming chocolate into universal shapes, such as hearts, flowers, teddy bears and spheres. I use two types of mould for the projects in this book: silicone rubber moulds for chocolate paste and plastic moulds for tempered chocolate. A huge variety of both types of moulds are available from sugarcraft suppliers (see pp. 118–119).

silicone rubber moulds

Silicone rubber moulds can be used with chocolate paste to instantly make a variety of shapes to decorate your creations. When working with chocolate paste, it is easiest to use shallow moulds with clear, defined detail, as it is often difficult to remove the paste from a deep mould that has a lot of detail. To use silicone rubber moulds, follow these simple steps:

1 Briefly knead a piece of chocolate paste with a little icing sugar.

2 Press the chocolate paste into the mould and gently bend the mould back to release the shape. The moulded shape can be attached to a cake using a little tempered chocolate (see p. 11).

To reduce stickiness, roll the chocolate paste in a little icing sugar

plastic moulds

Plastic moulds are so versatile and are great when working with tempered chocolate, as they provide a firmer foundation. With so many designs to choose from, you can let your imagination run wild – just follow these simple steps:

1 Temper your chocolate, following the instructions on p. 11.

2 Warm the mould gently using a dry heat.

3 Place the tempered chocolate in a disposable piping bag, and pipe into the clean, dry mould.

4 Tap the mould gently to allow any air bubbles to come to the surface.

5 Place the mould in the fridge to completely set for 20 minutes.

6 Carefully tip the mould up to release the moulded chocolate.

Add coloured cocoa butter to change the colour of your chocolates. White chocolate has a cream, not a white base, so by adding pink, your chocolate will turn peach!

lollipops

Lollipops are great fun to create in no time at all. They make fantastic gifts for children and adults alike and can even be used to dip into chocolate fondue as delicious treats to liven up a girls' night in. You can cover lollipops in foil for a professional touch, or make a batch of lollipops and present them in an embellished jar as a beautiful table centrepiece.

making lollipops

Lollipops are quick and very simple to make using tempered chocolate (see p. 11) and a lollipop mould of your choice. Refer to p. 27 for instructions on how to use moulds.

1 Temper the chocolate (see p. 11) and use a disposable piping bag to pipe it into lollipop moulds.

2 Quickly take a lollipop stick and lay it into the mould. Roll the stick so that it becomes completely covered in the chocolate. Tap the mould to allow any air bubbles to settle.

If your mould is detailed, dip a dry paintbrush into the chocolate and paint the surface of the mould, then add your chocolate in a disposable piping bag

3 Leave to dry for approximately 20 minutes in the fridge, then carefully remove the lollipop from the mould.

transfer sheets

Transfer sheets are acetate sheets that have an edible pattern embossed onto them with cocoa butter. When covered with tempered chocolate (see p. 11), the heat reacts with the cocoa butter to transfer the pattern onto the chocolate. Using transfer sheets is the easiest way to turn a plain surface into something unique. Available in a variety of colours and designs (see pp. 118–119 for Suppliers), transfer sheets can be used to decorate chocolate shards, to make cut out shapes or to wrap around cakes for dramatic effect.

transfer sheet tips

- Think carefully about which chocolate will best show off the design of your transfer sheet. The leopard print design (right) would not be visible on dark chocolate and the snowflake design (below right) would be lost using white chocolate.

- Transfer sheets have a single use only. Once the pattern has been printed onto the chocolate it will become a plain sheet of acetate.

- Transfer sheets should be stored in a cool dry place, away from sunlight to prevent any colour fade.

using transfer sheets

To create fantastic results with transfer sheets, follow these simple steps:

1 Lay a transfer sheet onto your work surface with the embossed cocoa butter print facing upwards.

2 Temper some chocolate (see p. 11) and pour it onto the sheet. Use a palette knife to spread the chocolate in an even, thin layer across the transfer sheet.

3 Allow the chocolate to dry completely then carefully remove the transfer sheet to leave the pattern imprinted onto the chocolate.

4 If you are making shards or shapes, wait for about 2–3 minutes for the chocolate to start to 'dull' then cut out your shapes. Leave to dry completely for approximately 20 minutes before removing the acetate sheet.

flowers

Chocolate flowers are so impressive and make a beautiful addition to any cake or cupcake. As chocolate paste is so pliable, it is easy to mould different types of flowers by varying the size, shape and number of the petals. I'm using roses, orchids and gerberas to brighten up the projects in this book, however you can use the making up instructions as a starting point for making up your own designs.

roses

Traditionally, roses are the most popular flower and when reworked in chocolate they are just as pretty and even more tempting! I used dark chocolate roses to add a delicately feminine touch to the Butterfly Beauty cake (see p. 62–65).

making up the roses
To create your own chocolate paste roses, follow these simple steps:

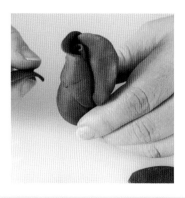

1 Roll out the chocolate paste onto icing sugar to approximately 3mm (⅛in) thick.

2 Cut out 11 petals using a metal rose petal cutter and create a cone of chocolate paste for the flower centre.

3 Gently pinch the edge of each petal to soften its appearance.

4 Begin attaching the petals. The first petal should be wrapped around the cone.

The chocolate paste should stick to itself and should not require any additional sugar glue or chocolate to hold it in place

5 The second and third petals are wrapped around the first, overlapping each other.

6 Attach the next three petals, overlapping each other to form the next layer.

7 The final layer will contain five petals. Once attached, gently bend the petals back for a realistic effect.

Don't re-roll the leftovers as they will become hot and sticky. Allow to cool in a plastic bag before re-using

orchids

These classic flowers replicated in white chocolate are just so pretty, it's no wonder they are the choice of the modern bride. Embellishing the petals with dusting powder gives the orchids a uniquely realistic touch.

making up the orchids

Creating orchids highlights just how versatile the chocolate paste can be.

1 Roll out some white chocolate paste onto icing sugar. Run a textured rolling pin over the paste.

2 Cut out five petal shapes, pinch the top of each and paint the centres with magenta dusting powder and alcohol. Lay to dry overnight on a cup-shaped piece of foil. The chocolate paste should stick to itself with no need for sugar glue.

3 Form the column of the orchid from white paste, cut out the throat and texture the edges. Place the column onto the throat and lay the flowers onto a former to dry overnight.

4 Paint the throat of the orchid using magenta dusting powder and alcohol, then dust under the column and sepals with magenta dusting powder.

5 Assemble the orchid in situ on the cake using a little tempered chocolate or cool spray.

important note:
Cool spray is a gas and when sprayed onto wet chocolate, sets it instantly. Cool spray is not recommended for consumption, therefore if used, the flowers should not be eaten. Alternatively, the orchids can be assembled using tempered chocolate (see p. 11). Place a small piece of sponge under the throat to hold the petals in position for 3–4 minutes until dry.

gerberas

Gerberas are so vibrant and make such striking displays, such as on the Sunny Delights cupcakes (see pp. 82–83). They are available in a fantastic range of colours and are guaranteed to brighten up your creations.

making up the gerberas

Creating gerberas is easy using a gerbera cutter (see Suppliers (poc) on p. 119) and following these simple steps:

1 Roll out some orange flavoured paste onto icing sugar to approximately 3mm (⅛in) thick. Dust the gerbera cutter in icing sugar then carefully cut out the flower shape.

2 Place the flowers onto a piece of foil, cupping the foil to give more of a 3D shape to the petals. Leave to dry overnight.

Simply vary the flavoured paste to experiment with a range of colours

3 Cut out a second flower. Pipe a small dot of ganache (see p. 21) into the centre of the first flower and place the second flower onto it.

4 Pipe a dot of ganache into the centre of the flower and leave to dry overnight at room temperature or for 2–3 hours in the fridge.

true love

cigarillos and curls

This luxurious chocolate cigarillo cake will make a mouth-watering centrepiece for an engagement party. It is easier to create than you would imagine; simply use dowels to stack four cakes together to form an impressive tower. Attaching chocolate cigarillos to a buttercream layer around the outside cleverly hides the layers, creating a striking, not-to-mention delicious cake that your guests will love!

The opulent purple and silver colour scheme complements the dark chocolate cake and the addition of silk flowers and a silver butterfly give the cake feminine appeal. This arrangement could easily be altered to suit a wedding colour scheme.

you will need ...

- ⚜ four 15.5cm (6in) round sponge cakes
- ⚜ 15.5cm (6in) thin round cake board
- ⚜ 700g (1lb 9oz) dark chocolate cigarillos
- ⚜ 300g (10½oz) dark chocolate curls (tc)
- ⚜ one batch of dark chocolate buttercream
- ⚜ 23cm (9in) white plate
- ⚜ five plastic dowels

  purple ribbon
- ⚜ purple silk flowers
- ⚜ silk butterfly
- ⚜ diamanté stems (cg)
- ⚜ flower pick (poc)

assembling

1 Prepare four 15.5cm (6in) round chocolate sponge cakes.

2 Place the first cake onto the white plate, securing with a spreading of chocolate buttercream. Spread a thin layer of chocolate buttercream onto the cake and place the second cake on top.

3 Place the third cake onto the cake board, securing with chocolate buttercream. Spread a thick layer of buttercream onto this cake and place the fourth cake on top. You should now have two cakes side-by-side, each measuring approximately 10cm (4in) in depth.

Add texture by densely scattering dark chocolate curls over the top of the cake to make the perfect base for your floral decorations.

4 Dowel the cakes on the white plate and cover with a layer of chocolate buttercream. Place a 15.5cm (6in) round disc of greaseproof paper onto this cake and spread a thin layer of chocolate buttercream on top. Dowel the other two cakes on the 15.5cm (6in) cake board and stack on top.

5 Coat the whole cake with a layer of chocolate buttercream to stabilize its structure.

decorating

1 Attach the dark chocolate cigarillos closely together around the bottom cake by pushing them into the buttercream coating. Repeat to attach the cigarillos to the top cake.

2 Scatter the chocolate curls densely over the top of the cake to create the textured topping.

3 Tie the purple ribbon around the whole cake to hide the join between the two layers of cigarillos.

4 Wind some diamanté stems around the ribbon bow and the silk flowers and arrange the silk flowers on top of the cake without inserting into the cake. Push the butterfly wire into a flower pick on the top of the cake.

Use a wide ribbon to hide the joins between the cigarillos and add a little sparkle with eye-catching diamanté stems.

Make this cake on a smaller scale by layering just two chocolate cakes together and decorating with a single layer of dark chocolate cigarillos

back to basics   basic tool kit p. 9 ... sponge pp. 16–17 ... dowelling pp. 14–15 ... buttercream p. 23 ...

silver sensation

This stunning white chocolate single-layered cake is perfect for celebrating a silver wedding anniversary. It is given a modern edge by decorating shards of white couverture chocolate with a contemporary metallic blue transfer sheet design and layering these shards around the outside of the cake. A sparkling blue crystal spray topper and decorative silver ribbon add a highly sophisticated finishing touch.

The icy blue of the chocolate shards contrasts dramatically with the white chocolate topping to create a cool, crisp effect that would be perfect for a winter wedding. To adapt the design for a golden wedding anniversary, use dark chocolate and golden embellishments.

you will need ...

- 🏵 **20cm (8in) round sponge cake**
- 🏵 **28cm (11in) round cake board**
- 🏵 **500g (1lb 2oz) white couverture chocolate (tc)**
- 🏵 **300g (10½oz) white chocolate curls (tc)**
- 🏵 **one batch of white chocolate buttercream**
- 🏵 **blue metallic swirl transfer sheet (tc)**
- 🏵 **silver ribbon (cg)**
- 🏵 **crystal spray (cg)**
- 🏵 **flower pick (poc)**

assembling

1 To make the chocolate shards, temper the white couverture chocolate and spread a thin, even layer onto the rough, patterned side of the transfer sheet. Use a palette knife to spread the chocolate evenly across the sheet.

2 Wait a few minutes for the chocolate to begin to set. Using a sharp knife cut out 15 shards, each measuring 6 x 5cm (2⅜ x 2in). Leave the shards to dry completely for 20 minutes before carefully peeling off the transfer sheet to reveal the pattern.

3 Prepare one 20cm (8in) round sponge cake and place onto the cake board. Spread a medium thick layer of chocolate buttercream around the cake and start to position the shards around the sides of the cake, overlapping each one.

The silver ribbon helps to hold the chocolate shards firmly in place, as well as giving the cake a stunning finishing touch.

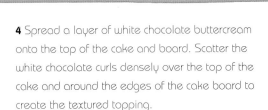

4 Spread a layer of white chocolate buttercream onto the top of the cake and board. Scatter the white chocolate curls densely over the top of the cake and around the edges of the cake board to create the textured topping.

decorating

1 Push a small flower pick into the centre of the cake, fill with a little white chocolate buttercream and place the crystal spray into the pick.

2 Tie the silver ribbon around the shards and attach to the edge of the cake board.

If you can't find a suitable crystal topper, lay some silver silk flowers on top of the cake

Densely scattering white chocolate curls on top of the cake creates a delightful texture. The delicate crystal spray adds an eye-catching sparkle to the finished design.

back to basics basic tool kit p. 9 ... tempering p. 11 ... sponge pp. 16–17 ... buttercream p. 23 ... transfer sheets pp. 30–31 ...

going for gold

Celebrate a golden wedding in style with this heavenly dark chocolate covered cake, elegantly decorated with embossed golden flowers and edible balls. As a single-layer cake it is quick to make and cover, allowing you plenty of time for the decoration, to ensure you make a big impression. This cake would also be perfect for a birthday celebration, embellished with simple gold candles.

These 3D gold flowers look so elegant and will really make a statement for a golden wedding celebration. Simple to create using a sugar cutter and flower mould, you could even use this design to decorate accompanying mini cakes or cookies.

you will need ...

- 15.5cm (6in) round chocolate cake
- 23cm (9in) cake drum
- 750g (1lb 10½oz) dark chocolate paste (tc)
- 25g (1oz) dark couverture chocolate (tc)
- 10 gold edible balls (poc)
- small pot of bright gold dusting powder (ea)
- flower mould (fpc)
- large flat floral cutter (lc)
- sugar gun with two nozzle shapes
- painting solution (ea)
- clear alcohol or cooled boiled water
- gold ribbon

assembling

1 Prepare one 15.5cm (6in) round chocolate sponge and cover with dark chocolate paste.

2 Run a textured rolling pin over the drum. Use a sugar gun with the largest nozzle to create a band of chocolate paste. Attach the band around the bottom of the cake using cooled boiled water or clear alcohol.

Running a textured rolling pin over the board creates a unique crinkled effect that resembles a fabric base, which is enhanced by the addition of gold ribbon.

decorating

1 Carefully press the large flower cutter into the cake until it embosses it. Use a paintbrush to apply a little cooled boiled water or clear alcohol around the outline of the flower. Repeat as desired over the cake.

2 Using the smallest nozzle, push the dark chocolate paste through the sugar gun. Attach the paste to the outline of the floral pattern, using a paintbrush to guide you.

3 Press some dark chocolate paste into the flower mould and allow to set.

4 Mix the bright gold dusting powder with the painting solution. Use this to carefully paint the flower's outline, centre and the cake board edge.

5 Temper the dark couverture chocolate and place into a piping bag. Attach the gold flower centres and edible gold balls to the cake using a little tempered chocolate.

6 Attach the ribbon to the edge of the cake board using a glue stick.

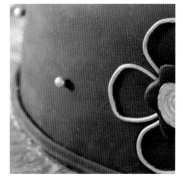

Gold colour can be added to the petal shapes with dusting powder and painting solution. Edible balls instantly add something special to the design.

Wait about an hour after you have covered your cake for the chocolate paste to cool down before embossing with the flower cutter

back to basics basic tool kit p. 9 ... tempering p. 11 ... paste pp. 12–13 ... sugar gun p. 24 ... moulds pp. 26–27 ...

from the heart

Give your heart on Valentine's Day and spoil that special someone by creating an individual cake or batch of cakes in a stylish presentation box.

you will need (for 16 mini cakes) ...

⚜ 16 heart-shaped mini cakes using 4 × 7.5cm (1½ × 3in) heart-shaped tins (sk)

⚜ 1kg (2lb 4oz) white chocolate paste

⚜ 75g (3oz) white couverture chocolate

⚜ one batch of chocolate buttercream

⚜ small pot of bright gold (ea) or poinsettia dusting powder (sk)

⚜ heart mould (fpc)

⚜ heart cutter (lc)

⚜ painting solution (ea)

⚜ gold ribbon

1 Cover each mini cake with a thin layer of chocolate buttercream. Roll out the white chocolate paste and carefully cover the cakes.

2 Temper a little white couverture chocolate and use this to attach the gold ribbon around the base of each cake.

3 Roll a small amount of white chocolate paste into a ball on icing sugar. Gently press into the heart mould using one large and one small heart shape. Remove the paste from the mould and carefully attach onto the cake with a little tempered chocolate.

4 Use the heart cutter to emboss the cake with a trailing heart pattern. Mix the bright gold or poinsettia dusting powder with a drop of painting solution and carefully fill in the embossed hearts.

back to basics basic tool kit p. 9 ... paste pp. 12–13 ... tempering p. 11 ... buttercream p. 23 ... moulds pp. 26–27 ...

fabulously floral

These 3D flowers will make the perfect Mother's Day gift, and what better way to print a design onto your chocolate creations than by using transfer sheets?

you will need ...

- ❀ five chocolate-covered bites
- ❀ 500g (1lb 2oz) white couverture chocolate
- ❀ two transfer sheets: orange blossom and chocolate daisies (tc)
- ❀ flower cutters (w)

1 Prepare five chocolate-covered bites. Temper 400g (14oz) of white couverture chocolate and spread a thin even layer onto the rough, patterned side of the transfer sheets.

2 Wait a few minutes until the chocolate begins to dull. Use the flower cutters to cut shapes from the tempered chocolate, making sure that the transfer sheets are kept in place.

3 Place the chocolate in the fridge for 20 minutes, or until firm.

4 Once the chocolate is set, carefully remove the backing from the transfer sheets.

5 Gently heat a sharp non-serrated knife with dry heat and use it to cut the chocolate into assorted shapes.

6 Temper the remaining 100g (4oz) of white couverture chocolate and place in a piping bag. Pipe onto the base of the bites and assemble the chocolate pieces as desired. Either arrange the flowers flat against the biscuits, or angle the chocolate shards for a 3D effect.

back to basics   basic tool kit p. 9 ... tempering p. 11 ... chocolate bites p. 20 ... transfer sheets pp. 30–31 ...

wedded bliss

white wedding

This wonderfully elegant wedding cake is traditional in shape, yet contemporary in design. The three tiers are coated in white chocolate and embellished with a stunning array of chocolate orchids. White chocolate beads are added around each cake layer to resemble beautiful strings of pearls. Embossed silver butterflies and silver ribbon look striking against the white chocolate and add a final touch of sparkle to the cake.

White chocolate orchids make a real statement on a simple tiered cake and will even complement your bridal bouquet. The details on the petals give the flowers a realistic touch, adding beauty to the cake.

you will need ...

- ❀ 10cm (4in), 15.5cm (6in) and 20cm (8in) round sponge cakes
- ❀ 10cm (4in) and 15.5cm (6in) thin round cake boards
- ❀ 28cm (11in) cake drum
- ❀ 1kg (2lb 3oz) white chocolate
- ❀ 3kg (6½lb) of white chocolate paste
- ❀ nine white chocolate orchids
- ❀ two batches of white chocolate buttercream
- ❀ ½ tsp Silver Snow (ea)
- ❀ ⅛ tsp painting solution (ea)
- ❀ black dusting powder
- ❀ small butterfly patchwork cutter (pc)
- ❀ beadmaker (poc)
- ❀ nine plastic dowels
- ❀ silver ribbon

assembling

1 Prepare the sponge cakes and fill with a layer of buttercream. Place each cake onto the relevant size board. The 20cm (8in) cake should be placed directly onto the 28cm (11in) cake drum.

2 Coat the outside of each sponge cake with the buttercream mixture. Cover the cakes with cling film and leave to stand for 30 minutes or until firm.

3 Knead the white chocolate paste until soft. If the paste is very hard, soften in the microwave for 10 seconds on full power.

Wait until the paste is completely dry before embossing or it will be too sticky

White chocolate beads give a lovely finish to the cake and are great for hiding the joins between the cake layers.

4 Roll out the white chocolate paste onto icing sugar and cover the cakes. Remove any excess icing sugar with a clean dry paintbrush.

5 Dowel the 15cm (6in) and 20cm (8in) cakes. Stack the three cakes together, offsetting them so that they are stacked towards the back to allow room to place the chocolate orchids.

These embossed butterflies are painted with edible silver food colouring to give a shimmering elegance to the cake.

decorating

1 Use a beadmaker to create a strip of white chocolate beads. Fix the beads in place around the circumference of each cake using a small amount of tempered white chocolate.

2 Prepare nine white chocolate orchids and use a little tempered white chocolate to attach the orchids across the front of the cake in a random pattern.

3 Once the chocolate paste has dried, emboss the butterfly cutter into the side of each cake, placing one butterfly on each layer.

4 Mix the Silver Snow with a small amount of black dusting powder to create edible silver food colouring. Apply with the painting solution to carefully fill in the embossed butterflies.

5 Use a glue stick to attach the silver ribbon to the edge of the cake board.

For sweet little wedding favours, use the orchids to decorate mini cakes

back to basics   basic tool kit p. 9 ... paste pp. 12–13 ... sponge pp. 16–17 ... dowelling pp. 14–15 ...
buttercream p.23 ... beadmaker p. 25 ... orchids pp. 34–35 ...

butterfly beauty

If you are looking for a chocolaty twist on a traditional floral wedding cake design, this is the cake for you. This two-tiered beauty is delicately feminine in style, adorned with a scattering of dark chocolate roses, pink blossoms and striking butterfly plaques. The sharpness of the plaque design, created simply by using a butterfly stencil and a little dark couverture chocolate, adds a truly professional touch.

Create a range of dark chocolate roses and cut tiny pink blossoms from strawberry flavoured paste to display creatively between the tiers. You could use the flowers to decorate white chocolate cupcakes or mini cakes to give as wedding favours.

you will need ...

- 15.5cm (6in) and 23cm (9in) round sponge cakes
- 15.5cm (6in) thin round cake board
- 28cm (11in) cake drum
- one batch of chocolate buttercream
- 1.75kg (4lb) white chocolate paste (tc)
- 150g (5½oz) strawberry paste (tc)
- 250g (9oz) dark chocolate paste (tc)
- 50g (1¾oz) white couverture chocolate
- 25g (1oz) dark couverture chocolate
- flower plaque cutter (w)
- butterfly stencil (lc)
- flower cutters and blossom plunger cutters (poc)
- five plastic dowels
- dark brown ribbon (cg)

assembling

1 Prepare the 15.5cm (6in) round sponge cake and place onto the 15.5cm (6in) thin round cake board. Prepare the 23cm (9in) round sponge cake and place onto the 28cm (11in) round cake drum. Spread a thin layer of buttercream over both cakes and cover with white chocolate paste.

2 Place five equally cut dowels into the 23cm (9in) cake to support the 15.5cm (6in) cake. Spread a little tempered white chocolate onto the 23cm (9in) cake and place the 15.5cm (6in) cake on top.

3 Paint the cake board with some clear alcohol or cooled boiled water. Roll out a long strip of white chocolate paste and attach to the board. Create marks using a textured rolling pin all around the chocolate paste. Cut off any excess paste with a plastic side scraper.

4 Knead a small amount of dark chocolate paste and load into a sugar gun. Pipe two thin strips – one to cover the join between the base of the two cakes and one for the base of the larger cake. Attach the dark chocolate paste strips with cool boiled water or clear alcohol.

The simplicity of the strawberry paste blossoms contrasts beautifully against the three-dimensional dark chocolate roses.

decorating

1 Roll out some white chocolate paste and cut out two petal plaques using the flower plaque cutter. Leave in the fridge for a few hours or overnight to allow the paste to harden.

2 Place the butterfly stencil onto the plaque. Gently spread a thin layer of tempered dark chocolate over the stencil in one swift motion, remove the stencil immediately and leave for 20 minutes to dry. Attach the butterfly plaques to the cake using tempered white chocolate.

3 Knead a small amount of dark chocolate paste and load into the sugar gun. Using a paintbrush, wet the outer edges of the plaque with a little water. Squeeze the chocolate paste through the gun and guide it onto the edges of the plaque with a dry paintbrush.

4 Roll out the strawberry flavoured paste onto icing sugar and use the cutters to cut out assorted blossom sizes. Attach the blossoms to the cake with a little water and indent the centre of each flower with a cocktail stick.

This pretty plaque is created using a butterfly stencil. Use a different stencil design if you prefer, e.g. a delicate flower design would enhance the floral effect.

For a quick alternative, attach silk roses onto the sides of the cake

5 Prepare nine dark chocolate roses in assorted sizes. Attach the roses to the cake with a little tempered white chocolate.

6 Attach the brown ribbon to the edges of the cake board using a glue stick.

back to basics   basic tool kit p. 9 ... paste pp. 12–13 ... dowelling pp. 14–15 ... buttercream p. 23 ... sugar gun p. 24 ... roses pp. 32–33 ...

blossom delights

These pretty pastel mini cakes look stunning when prepared individually or grouped on a large plate as a fun alternative to the traditional wedding cake.

you will need ...

- ❀ four chocolate mini cakes
- ❀ 250g (9oz) dark chocolate paste (tc)
- ❀ 250g (9oz) strawberry flavoured paste (tc)
- ❀ 100g (3½oz) dark couverture chocolate
- ❀ icing sugar
- ❀ blossom plunger flower cutters (poc)
- ❀ chocolate brown ribbon (cg)
- ❀ pink ribbon (cg)

1 Prepare the mini cakes. Roll out the strawberry flavoured chocolate paste over plenty of icing sugar and cover the mini cakes, removing any excess icing sugar with a clean dry paintbrush.

2 Attach the pink and brown ribbon around the bases of the mini cakes.

3 Roll out the dark chocolate flavoured paste onto icing sugar. Dip the blossom plunge cutter into the icing sugar and cut out a flower.

4 Pipe a tiny dot of tempered chocolate onto the mini cake then attach the flower from the cutter. Repeat to create a blossom pattern around the top of the cake.

5 Pipe dots of tempered chocolate or add tiny rolled pieces of strawberry flavoured paste to form the flower centres.

Mix and match by covering the cakes in dark chocolate paste and adding flowers cut from strawberry paste

back to basics basic tool kit p. 9 ... tempering p. 11 ... paste pp. 12–13 ...

floral centrepiece

These sweet little lollipops are guaranteed to make your guests smile! They make wonderful table centrepieces or can be given as cute individual wedding favours.

you will need ...

- 🌸 150g (5oz) white couverture chocolate
- 🌸 2 tsp pink cocoa butter (k)
- 🌸 2 tsp orange cocoa butter (k)
- 🌸 flower mould (hc)
- 🌸 lollipop sticks (k)
- 🌸 glass jars
- 🌸 clear plastic beads
- 🌸 organza ribbon

1 Take a bottle of coloured cocoa butter, ensure the lid is open and heat in the microwave on full power for 30 seconds. Shake the bottle and repeat the process until the cocoa butter has melted. Polish the flower mould before use with a piece of kitchen roll.

2 Temper the white chocolate and place in a piping bag. Cut the end off the bag and carefully pipe the centres of the flowers. Place in the fridge for 5 minutes or until the chocolate sets.

3 Mix some of the coloured cocoa butter with the white chocolate and pipe the chocolate into the mould. Gently tap the mould against your work surface to bring any bubbles to the surface. Lay the lollipop stick into the chocolate and place in the fridge to set for approximately 20 minutes.

4 To create the centrepiece, fill a glass jar with clear plastic beads to support the sticks and add enough lollipops for the guests at the table. Tie a matching organza ribbon around the centre and add a string of glass beads around the top of the jar.

back to basics basic tool kit p. 9 ... tempering p. 11 ... moulds pp. 26–27 ... lollipops pp. 28–29 ...

tempting truffles

These delicious truffles are quick to create and will make the perfect wedding favour when presented in a stylish box or gift bag.

you will need (for 15 truffles) ...

- ❀ one batch of ganache
- ❀ 50g (1¾oz) dark couverture chocolate
- ❀ 25g (1oz) white couverture chocolate (tc)

1 Allow the ganache to cool for about 30 minutes at room temperature. Make 15 balls approximately 2½cm (1in) in diameter by rolling strips of ganache. Place the balls on a greaseproof sheet and allow to harden completely.

2 Temper the dark couverture chocolate and dip the balls into the tempered chocolate. Remove the balls with a fork and tap them onto the edge of the bowl to remove any excess chocolate and air bubbles. Place the truffles onto an acetate sheet and leave to dry for approximately 30 minutes.

3 Temper the white couverture chocolate, place in a disposable piping bag and drizzle over the truffles. Leave for 10 minutes until dry.

Roll the truffles in cocoa powder for a tasty alternative topping

back to basics   basic tool kit p. 9 ... tempering p. 11 ... ganache p. 21 ...

birthday treats

born to be wild

What do you get for the girl who has everything on her special day?
If she already has the outfit, the shoes and the handbag, she is sure to
adore this highly fashionable leopard print cake to complete her collection.
Using a contemporary leopard print transfer sheet design instantly transfers
a plain two-tiered cake into a high-impact statement and a beautiful rose
corsage adds feminine charm to the design.

The dark brown and cream
colour scheme not only
shows off the colours of
the season, but also really
makes this bold design
stand out from the crowd.

you will need ...

- 🌸 15cm (6in) and 10cm (4in) square chocolate cake
- 🌸 10cm (4in) thin square cake board
- 🌸 23cm (9in) square cake drum
- 🌸 one batch of chocolate buttercream
- 🌸 1kg (2lb 4oz) white chocolate paste (tc)
- 🌸 250g (9oz) dark chocolate paste (tc)
- 🌸 250g (9oz) white couverture chocolate (tc)
- 🌸 leopard print transfer sheet (tc)
- 🌸 four plastic dowels
- 🌸 rose petal cutter
- 🌸 2cm (¾in) round cutter
- 🌸 sugar gun (pc)
- 🌸 cooled boiled water
- 🌸 brown ribbon (cg)

Preparing the rose

1 Cut out ten rose petals from dark chocolate paste. Use the textured rolling pin to frill each petal.

2 To form the flower shape, overlap the five outside petals then add a second inner row of another five petals. The chocolate paste petals will stick to each other to hold the rose shape. Leave the flower to dry for 2–3 hours.

Use a textured rolling pin to frill the edges of each rose petal to create a realistically moulded flower.

assembling the cake

1 Prepare the 10cm (4in) square chocolate cake and place onto the 10cm (4in) thin cake board. Prepare the 15cm (6in) square chocolate cake and place onto the 23cm (9in) square cake drum.

2 Spread a thick layer of buttercream over each cake and cover with white chocolate paste.

3 Push four equally cut dowels into the 15cm (6in) cake to support the weight of the smaller cake. Apply a thin layer of tempered chocolate and place the 10cm (4in) cake on top of the 15cm (6in) cake.

4 Cover the cake board with a long strip of chocolate paste then roll the textured rolling pin over it. Cut off any excess paste with a plastic side scraper.

the leopard print pattern

1 Cut out the leopard print transfer sheet to fit the cake, measuring from the base of the larger cake over the top of the 10cm (4in) cake. This should measure approximately 32 × 10cm (12½ × 4in).

2 Temper the white chocolate and spread a thin even layer onto the rough, patterned side of the transfer sheet. While the chocolate is still wet, carefully attach the transfer sheet to the cake, starting from the front base of the bottom cake.

3 Spread a small amount of chocolate onto the rough, patterned side of a separate leopard print transfer sheet. Wait a couple of minutes until the chocolate begins to harden, then cut out a 2cm (¾in) round shape. Leave to dry for 20 minutes. Once the chocolate has set, remove the backing from the transfer sheets to reveal the pattern.

4 Knead some dark chocolate paste and load into the sugar gun. Squeeze the gun to pipe a line of paste around the base of each cake. Attach the paste with a little cool boiled water and a paintbrush.

5 Position the centre of the flower with some tempered chocolate, then attach to the cake. Glue the brown ribbon to the edge of the cake board.

Adding ribbon around the edge of the cake board creates the perfect finishing touch.

If any excess chocolate leaks when you attach the transfer sheet, quickly remove with a paintbrush

back to basics   basic tool kit p. 9 ... tempering p. 11 ... paste pp. 12–13 ... dowelling pp. 14–15 ... sponge pp. 16–17 ... buttercream p.23 ... sugar gun p. 24 ... transfer sheets pp. 30–31 ...

chocolate explosion

This erupting chocolate volcano certainly has the wow factor and makes a great party cake for any age, from a children's birthday party to a 50th celebration. Form the basic shape by cutting and dowelling various sizes of sponge cake layers before covering with chocolate flakes to create an interesting texture. Chocolate balls fall from the top and scatter down the sides of the cake for a dramatic effect.

Create the fiery orange chocolate balls by adding orange cocoa butter to tempered white couverture chocolate and pouring into moulds. The orange colour swirls into the white chocolate to create a marble effect that is perfect for representing volcanic lava.

you will need...

- 15cm (6in), 20cm (8in) and 25cm (10in) round cakes
- 15cm (6in) and 25cm (10in) round thin cake boards
- 37.5cm (15in) round cake drum
- 300g (11½oz) white couverture chocolate (tc)
- 300g (11½oz) milk couverture chocolate (tc)
- four batches of chocolate buttercream
- 125 chocolate flakes
- orange cocoa butter
- 50 chocolate balls
- 3cm (1⅜in) and 4cm (1½in) half sphere polycarbonate moulds (hc)
- brown ribbon (cg)
- nine plastic dowels

making the orange chocolate balls

1 You will need to make up seven 4cm (1½in) and thirty 3cm (1⅜in) balls. Temper 300g (11½oz) of white couverture chocolate, add 6 tsp of orange cocoa butter and swirl the colour into the chocolate to create a marble effect.

2 Pour the chocolate into the half sphere moulds. Tap the moulds on the work surface to disperse any air bubbles, tip the whole mould upside down and allow any excess chocolate to drip out. Tap the side of the moulds and scrape off any excess chocolate. Place the moulds in the fridge to set for approximately 20 minutes.

3 Once the balls have set, remove the chocolate from the moulds then join the two halves of the balls together either with a little tempered chocolate or by melting the edges on a warm surface.

assembling the cake

1 Prepare the 15cm (6in), 20cm (8in) and 25cm (10in) round sponge cakes. To stack the cake, take the 25cm (10in) cake and cut it in half horizontally. Place one half onto the 37.5cm (15in) round cake drum and spread a thick layer of chocolate buttercream onto it.

Clusters of orange chocolate balls and smaller chocolate balls spill from the top and down the sides of the cake for a striking look.

2 Cut the other half of the 25cm (10in) cake down to a 23cm (9in) round and place it centrally onto the 25cm (10in) round cake. Place five equally cut dowels into the cake ready to support the next cake. Spread a thin layer of buttercream onto the top of the dowelled cake.

3 Cut the 23cm (9in) cake in half horizontally, place one half onto a 20cm (8in) cake board and position onto the dowels. Cut the other half of the 20cm (8in) cake down to an 18cm (7in) round cake. Spread a thick layer of buttercream onto the 20cm (8in) cake and place the 18cm (7in) cake on top. Dowel this cake as described above.

4 Spread a thin layer of buttercream onto the dowelled cake, cut the 15cm (6in) cake in half horizontally and place one half onto a 15cm (6in) cake board, and onto the dowels. Cut the other half of this cake down to a 12.5cm (5in) round cake.

5 Spread a thick layer of buttercream onto the 15cm (6in) cake and place the 12.5cm (5in) cake centrally onto the cake. Trim the whole structure with a knife.

Take your time when stacking the layers together and use a knife to carefully trim the edges for a smooth structure.

decorating

1 Coat the whole cake in chocolate buttercream and stick the chocolate flakes onto the cake, starting at the bottom of the cake.

2 With a sharp knife, score the cake board in different directions. Temper the milk chocolate and apply to the board with a paintbrush.

3 With the remaining tempered chocolate, attach the orange and milk chocolate balls to the volcano. Glue the brown ribbon to the cake board.

back to basics   basic tool kit p. 9 ... tempering p. 11 ... dowelling pp. 14–15 ... sponge pp. 16–17 ... buttercream p. 23 ... moulds pp. 26–27 ...

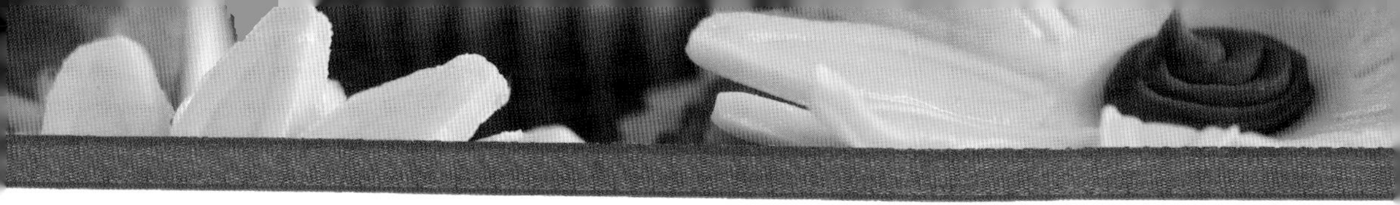

sunny delights

These vibrant cupcakes are beautifully decorated with brightly coloured gerberas, guaranteed to make a bright and bold statement at any birthday party.

you will need
(for 12 cakes) ...

❀ one batch of cupcakes

❀ 120g (4¼oz) of ganache

❀ 12 orange gerberas

❀ orange paper cases (poc)

1 Prepare 12 cupcakes. Carefully spoon some of the ganache onto each cupcake until it is level with the top of the paper case.

2 Gently tap the cupcake onto your work surface to enable any air bubbles to rise to the surface. Allow to settle for a few minutes, adding more ganache if required.

3 Make up 12 gerberas and carefully place onto the ganache. Leave to dry for 2–3 hours.

Refer to pp. 32–35 for further floral inspiration to decorate your cupcakes

back to basics   basic tool kit p. 9 ... cupcakes p. 18 ... ganache p. 21 ... gerberas pp. 36–37 ...

baby's first birthday

These adorable mini cakes are ideal for celebrating baby's first birthday or make to give as sweet christening gifts.

you will need (for 16 mini cakes) ...

- 16 sponge cakes, 5 × 3.75cm (2 × 1½in)
- 200g (7oz) white couverture chocolate (tc)
- 750g (1lb 8oz) white chocolate paste (tc)
- one batch of chocolate buttercream
- pink cocoa butter (k)
- teddy mould (hc)
- 1.5cm (⅝in) circle cutter (poc)
- peach ribbon (cg)

1 Spread an even, thin layer of buttercream carefully onto each cake. Roll out the white chocolate paste and use this to cover the cakes.

2 To turn the chocolate peach, temper the white chocolate, add 5 tsp of pink cocoa butter to the tempered chocolate and mix thoroughly. If you want a stronger colour, add more pink cocoa butter, one teaspoon at a time.

3 Pour the tempered chocolate into a piping bag and pipe the chocolate into the bite-size teddy mould to make 16 teddies. Tap the mould to disperse any bubbles and leave to dry in the fridge for approximately 20 minutes.

4 Spread the remaining chocolate onto food grade acetate sheets and leave to set for a few minutes. For each cake cut out eight coloured discs with the circle cutter and leave for 20 minutes to dry completely.

5 Attach the ribbon, coloured discs and teddy decoration to each cake using a little tempered chocolate.

back to basics basic tool kit p. 9 ... tempering p. 11 ... paste pp. 12–13 ... sponge pp. 16–17 ... buttercream p. 23 ... moulds pp. 26–27 ...

chocolate jewels

These sparkly chocolate jewels are so quick and easy to create and make an impressive birthday treat for your family and friends.

you will need
(for 15 jewels) ...

- 125g (4½oz) dark couverture chocolate
- fine powder spray: gold and scarlet (k)
- 3D jewel mould (hc)

1 Temper 125g (4½oz) of dark couverture chocolate.

2 Place the tempered chocolate in a disposable piping bag and fill the chocolate moulds. Tap on the work surface to bring the air bubbles to the surface and leave to set in the fridge for approximately 20 minutes.

3 Carefully tap the chocolates out onto a piece of kitchen roll and spray randomly using the fine powder spray.

Wear cotton gloves when placing the chocolate in boxes to avoid the spray smudging

back to basics basic tool kit p. 9 ... tempering p. 11 ... moulds p. 26–27 ...

festive
indulgence

chocolate wreath

This luxurious wreath cake is similar in appearance to a traditional Christmas cake, but with a rich and chocolaty twist! Decadently decorated with white chocolate Christmas roses and dark chocolate holly leaves and finished with a sparkly ribbon, it makes an exciting alternative to an iced fruitcake. It will brighten up your festive spread or make a desirable centrepiece at a Christmas party.

Create beautiful Christmas roses from white chocolate paste and integrate with dark chocolate holly leaves and cigarillos for a contemporary wreath effect. The holly berries look so effective when coated with frosted flame dusting powder.

you will need ...

- ❀ 20cm (8in) round chocolate cake
- ❀ 28cm (11in) round cake drum
- ❀ 1kg (2lb 4oz) milk chocolate paste (tc)
- ❀ 250g (9oz) dark chocolate paste (tc)
- ❀ 100g (3½oz) white chocolate paste (tc)
- ❀ 25g (1oz) dark couverture chocolate
- ❀ one batch of chocolate buttercream
- ❀ 9 dark chocolate cigarillos
- ❀ flower cutter (op)
- ❀ holly cutter
- ❀ bright gold and frosted flame dusting powder (ea)
- ❀ sugar gun
- ❀ gold ribbon 4cm (1½in), 1.5cm (⅝in) and 3mm (⅛in) (cg)

assembling

1 Prepare the 20cm (8in) round chocolate cake and place onto the 28cm (11in) round drum. Spread a thick layer of buttercream over the cake and cover with milk chocolate paste.

2 Roll out a long strip of chocolate paste, paint a little cooled boiled water onto the cake board and attach the paste. Use a textured rolling pin to make a pattern around the edge and cut off any excess chocolate paste with a plastic side scraper.

decorating

1 Roll out 200g (7oz) of dark chocolate paste onto some icing sugar and use a medium metal holly cutter to cut out 35 holly leaves. Mark the veins of the holly with a Dresden tool and leave to dry for about 10 minutes.

2 Roll out 100g (3½oz) of white chocolate paste and use the flower cutter to cut out five white flowers. Frill the edges of each flower using a textured rolling pin and leave to dry for approximately 10 minutes.

Tie groups of cigarillos together with fine gold ribbon to resemble clusters of festive cinnamon sticks.

3 Load the sugar gun with a small amount of white chocolate paste. Squeeze the gun then remove a little paste with a Dresden tool and place into the centre of each flower. Dust the centre with some bright gold dusting powder.

4 Gently heat a sharp knife with some dry heat and use to carefully cut the cigarillos in half. Arrange three cigarillos together and tie with the 3mm (⅛in) gold ribbon.

5 Roll some dark chocolate paste into small balls for the holly berries and dust with frosted flame dusting powder.

6 Temper 25g (1oz) of dark couverture chocolate, place in a disposable piping bag and use to attach the holly, berries, Christmas rose and cigarillos in a wreath formation.

7 Tie the 4cm (1½in) ribbon around the cake and finish with a bow. Attach the 1.5cm (⅝in) ribbon to the edge of the cake board.

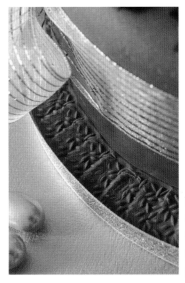

Tie thick gold organza ribbon around the base of the cake for perfect presentation.

The holly leaves and berries would look stunning as a mini cake decoration

back to basics   basic tool kit p. 9 … tempering p. 11 … paste pp. 12–13 … sponge pp. 16–17 … buttercream p.23… sugar gun p. 24 …

snowflake cups

For the ultimate indulgence this Christmas, spoil yourself with these luxurious chocolate mini cakes. The smooth surface of the dark chocolate cup contrasts dramatically with the textured topping, which conceals the rich, tempting cake within. Beautifully decorated with snowflakes and a sparkling gem topper, these cups look simply divine presented on a plate with raspberries or with a scoop of your favourite ice cream. The perfect way to end your Christmas meal!

A wide variety of transfer sheet patterns are available, so you can easily vary the design to suit any occasion. A floral pattern on a white chocolate base would be lovely for a Mother's Day treat, or you could use a heart design to celebrate Valentine's Day.

you will need
(for six mini cakes) ...

- six mini cakes: 4cm (1½in) high and 5cm (2in) in diameter
- 500g (1lb 2oz) dark chocolate
- 750g (1lb 10½oz) dark chocolate paste (tc)
- 300g (11oz) dark chocolate curls (tc)
- one snowflake transfer sheet (tc)
- 6 flower gems (cg)
- 6 flower picks (poc)

assembling

1 Prepare the mini cakes and cover with dark chocolate paste.

2 Measure the circumference of the mini cake. Calculate the area needed for the transfer sheet by adding an extra 2.5cm (1in) to the height and 2cm (¾in) to the width of the cake to allow for an overlap. Carefully cut out the transfer sheet.

3 Temper the dark chocolate and pour onto the rough side of the transfer sheet. Use a palette knife to spread the chocolate evenly across the sheet.

White snowflakes look really striking against the dark chocolate base. The glistening flower gem complements the snowflakes, adding eyecatching appeal to the mini cakes.

4 After a minute, pick up the transfer sheet and wrap it around the mini cake, allowing it to overlap at the back.

5 Place the cake in the fridge for approximately 20 minutes or until set. When the chocolate has hardened, carefully remove the backing from the transfer sheet to reveal the snowflake pattern.

decorating

1 Insert a small flower pick into the centre of the cake, fill with a little dark chocolate paste and place the flower gem into the pick.

2 Fill the top of the cake with dark chocolate curls and present as desired.

You could use the same method to cover a larger cake for a Christmas party

Chocolate curls make an easy and effective topping. If you don't want to buy them, simply use a grater to shave curls from a block of chocolate.

back to basics   basic tool kit p. 9 ... tempering p. 11 ... sponge pp. 16–17 ... transfer sheets pp. 30–31 ...

tempting tree hangings

These hanging treats are so quick and easy to create in a variety of festive shapes, but be warned, they won't stay on your tree for long!

you will need ...

- 🌼 1kg (2lb 3oz) white chocolate
- 🌼 two transfer sheets: holly, red gingham (tc)
- 🌼 metal round cutters: 6.5cm (2½in) and 1cm (⅜in) in diameter (poc)
- 🌼 metal holly cutter
- 🌼 3mm (⅛in) gold ribbon (cg)

1 Temper the white chocolate and spread an even layer onto the rough, patterned side of the holly and red gingham transfer sheets.

2 Wait a few minutes until the chocolate begins to dull. Use the large round cutter and holly metal cutters to carefully cut shapes out of the chocolate, making sure that the transfer sheets are kept in place.

3 Use the small round cutter to cut out a disc at the top of each shape. Place the chocolate in the fridge to set for 20 minutes, or until the chocolate is firm.

4 Once the chocolate is set, carefully remove the backing from the transfer sheets. Tie decorative ribbon through the small round holes and hang from the tree.

Experiment by varying the cutter shapes, the type of chocolate and even the transfer sheet pattern

back to basics   basic tool kit p. 9 ... tempering p. 11... transfer sheets pp. 30–31...

chocolate treasures

Children won't be able to keep their hands off these tempting chocolate coins. Why not add some peppermint essence to create tasty after-dinner mints so that adults can enjoy them too?

you will need (for 20 coins)...

- ⚜ 100g (3½oz) tempered chocolate of your choice
- ⚜ coin mould (hc)
- ⚜ assorted foils (k)

1 Polish the coin mould before use with a piece of kitchen roll. Temper the chocolate and place in a piping bag. Cut the end off the bag and fill the mould with chocolate.

2 Gently tap the mould against your work surface to bring any bubbles to the surface and allow the tempered chocolate to settle.

3 Place the mould in the fridge for 20 minutes to set. Once the chocolate has hardened, remove from the mould and wrap in coloured foil.

Wrap the coins in cellophane packaging and tie with a ribbon to create striking stocking fillers

back to basics   basic tool kit p. 9 ... tempering p. 11... moulds pp. 26–27...

star of wonder

These sparkly chocolate bites will make perfect treats for the stars in your life this Christmas. Serve on a platter at a party or tie together with ribbon as a classy gift.

**you will need
(for nine bites) ...**

- ❀ one batch of chocolate bites, 6cm (2⅜in) in diameter
- ❀ 250g (9oz) white chocolate paste (tc)
- ❀ 25g (1oz) dark couverture chocolate (tc)
- ❀ large star cutter
- ❀ disco white hologram edible cake glitter (ea)
- ❀ red dusting spray (k)

1 Prepare a batch of chocolate covered bites. Evenly roll out 250g (9oz) of white chocolate paste onto icing sugar and use the large star cutter to cut out nine star shapes.

2 Spray some of the white chocolate paste stars with the red dusting spray and dust the remainder with the disco white hologram edible cake glitter.

3 Temper 25g (1oz) of dark couverture chocolate and place in a disposable piping bag. Pipe a small dot of tempered chocolate onto the top of the chocolate bites and position a star on top. Pipe another dot of tempered chocolate onto this star and arrange the second star in a contrasting pattern, alternating between red and gold stars for interest.

For tasty stocking fillers, tie a stack of three biscuits together with an organza ribbon

back to basics   basic tool kit p. 9 ... tempering p. 11 ... paste pp. 12–13 ... chocolate bites p. 20 ...

more excuses

easter extravagance

Who could resist this sweet little chick nesting on top of a cute and contemporary Easter cake? Simply made up from white chocolate paste, she sits contently on her nest of chocolate flakes, guarding the white chocolate eggs from prying hands. The cake is decorated with circles of chocolate paste in springtime colours and green gingham ribbon adds a fresh finishing touch.

This little chick has such character that children and adults alike will adore her. The gold eggs are simple to make and are tempting treats for children; present in a simple bag tied with gingham ribbon.

you will need ...

- 20cm (8in) round chocolate cake
- 25cm (10in) round cake drum
- 150g (5½oz) white couverture chocolate
- 1kg (2lb 4oz) white chocolate paste (tc)
- 100g (3½oz) dark chocolate paste (tc)
- one batch chocolate buttercream
- 10 chocolate flakes
- orange paste food colouring (poc)
- green and yellow cocoa butter (k)
- 1.5cm (⅝in) round metal cutter
- food grade acetate sheets
- mini easter egg mould (hc)
- gold foils (f)
- cooled boiled water
- green check, lime green and gold ribbon (cg)

assembling the cake

1 Prepare the 20cm (8in) round chocolate cake and place onto the 25cm (10in) round cake drum. Spread a thin layer of buttercream all over the cake and cover with white chocolate paste.

2 Roll out the dark chocolate paste into a long strip. Paint the board with cool boiled water. Attach the chocolate paste, roll the textured rolling pin over it and remove any excess paste with a plastic side scraper.

3 Temper 50g (1¾oz) of white couverture chocolate and divide equally into two bowls. Add 2 tsp of yellow cocoa butter to one bowl and 2 tsp of green cocoa butter to the other. Mix the colours in, then spread them onto the separate sheets of acetate.

4 Wait approximately 2 minutes for the chocolate to start to set. Use the round metal cutter to cut out about 20 circles from both the yellow and green coloured chocolate. Leave to dry for 20 minutes.

Add green and yellow cocoa butter to tempered white chocolate to create a fresh, springtime tint.

forming the eggs

1 Temper the remaining white couverture chocolate, place in a disposable piping bag and pipe into the mini easter egg mould.

2 Tap the mould on the work surface to bring all the air bubbles to the surface. Leave to dry for 20 minutes. Release the eggs from the mould, place two halves together and wrap them in gold foil.

creating the chick

1 Roll out two balls of white chocolate paste, one slightly larger for the body. Place the smaller ball onto the larger ball.

2 Knead some white chocolate paste and load up the sugar gun. Squeeze the gun then use a Dresden tool to carefully remove short pieces of paste.

3 Attach the small pieces of paste to the chick to form the feathered texture. The paste will stick to itself and should not require additional adhesive.

4 Once the two balls are covered, roll a tiny piece of dark chocolate paste to form the eyes and use the Dresden tool to position them in place.

To save time, you could use pre-bought chocolate eggs to decorate the nest.

5 Colour a small amount of white chocolate paste with orange paste food colouring to form a beak.

preparing the nest

1 Arrange ten chocolate flakes to form a nest and stick them together using tempered chocolate.

2 Place the chick into the nest and arrange the eggs around it.

3 Attach the coloured chocolate discs to the cake using a little tempered white chocolate.

4 Attach the ribbon onto the edge of the cake board using a glue stick.

back to basics   basic tool kit p. 9 ... tempering p. 11 ... paste pp. 12–13 ... buttercream p. 23 ... sugar gun p. 24 ...

rich chocolate cups

Whether it's for a birthday, wedding, dinner party or simply a girls' night in, you won't need an excuse to make up these delicious delicacies.

you will need (for 12 chocolate cups) ...

- 🌼 25 × 25cm (10 × 10in) square sheet of chocolate sponge cake
- 🌼 12 dark chocolate cases (tc)
- 🌼 350g (12oz) ganache
- 🌼 12 dark chocolate truffles
- 🌼 12 white chocolate cigarillos
- 🌼 set of round metal cutters (poc)

1 Prepare a 25 × 25cm (10 × 10in) square sheet of chocolate cake. Use the round, metal cutter to cut out 12 chocolate cakes to fill the dark chocolate cases.

2 Pour the ganache into the chocolate cases. Gently tap the cups on the work surface to allow the ganache to settle. Add additional ganache until it is level with the top of the cake.

3 Prepare 12 truffles and place each truffle carefully onto the ganache. Gently twist a white chocolate cigarillo into the cake at an angle.

4 Leave to set at room temperature for approximately 2 hours.

Be careful not to overheat the ganache or it may melt the chocolate cases

back to basics basic tool kit p. 9 ... sponge pp. 16–17 ... ganache p. 21 ... truffles p. 22 ...

brownie points

Say thank you to that special someone with these scrumptious brownies. They will also make a well-deserved treat to celebrate Mother's Day.

you will need (for nine brownies) ...

- ✿ one batch of brownies, cut into 6cm (2⅜in) squares
- ✿ 50g (1¾oz) dark, milk and white chocolate paste (tc)
- ✿ 25g (1oz) dark couverture chocolate (tc)
- ✿ 25g white couverture chocolate (tc)

1 To make the dark and milk chocolate bows, roll out the dark and milk chocolate paste and cut into 1cm (⅜in) diameter strips.

2 Temper the dark chocolate and pipe a little onto the brownie to attach the chocolate paste strips.

3 Take two equal strips of paste and fold them over until they meet in the middle to form the bow. Attach the bow to the brownie then cut a smaller piece of paste to lay over the centre of the bow.

4 Temper 10g (¼oz) of white chocolate, place in a disposable piping bag and carefully pipe tiny dots onto the bows.

For the white chocolate bows, create white chocolate paste strips and pipe dots using tempered dark chocolate

back to basics basic tool kit p. 9 ... tempering p. 11 ... paste pp. 12–13 ... brownies p. 19 ...

stick on a smile

These cheerful white chocolate lollipops decorated with red, white and blue ribbons make a great treat for your 4th July celebrations.

you will need (for four giant lollipops) ...

- 600g (1lb 5oz) white couverture chocolate (tc)
- 40g (1½oz) dark chocolate paste (tc)
- lollipop mould (hc)
- 4 lollipop sticks (k)
- red, white and blue ribbon
- sugar gun

1 Temper the white couverture chocolate and place into a disposable piping bag. Cut the end off the bag and fill the lollipop mould.

2 Place the lollipop stick into the tempered chocolate and roll it to coat it evenly. Tap the mould gently onto the work surface to disperse any air bubbles. Leave in the fridge to set for approximately 20 minutes then remove from the mould.

3 Knead the dark chocolate paste for a few seconds until it becomes tacky and place it into the sugar gun with the smallest nozzle in place. Squeeze the sugar gun until it makes a long string of chocolate paste to form the smile and use a paintbrush to guide the paste into place. The paste should stick to the lollipop.

4 Roll two tiny balls of paste to form the eyes and press onto the lollipop. Tie the ribbons around the lollipop stick.

Arrange a few lollipops in a glass or small vase to create a fun table centrepiece

back to basics   basic tool kit p. 9 ... tempering p. 11 ... paste pp. 12–13 ... lollipops pp. 28–29 ...

fondue fun

Liven up a girls' night in by dipping these heart lollipops into melted dark chocolate and coating with chocolate curls for pure chocolate indulgence.

you will need (for 14 lollipops) ...

- ❀ 300g (11oz) dark couverture chocolate (tc)
- ❀ 200g (7oz) white couverture chocolate (tc)
- ❀ 200g (7oz) chocolate curls
- ❀ chocolate heart mould
- ❀ 14 lollipop sticks

1 Temper the white couverture chocolate, place into a disposable piping bag and pipe into the heart moulds.

2 Roll the lollipop sticks into the tempered white chocolate to coat them evenly and leave to dry in the fridge for approximately 20 minutes.

3 Melt the dark couverture chocolate ready for dipping, sprinkle the curls onto the plate and enjoy!

Why not make dark chocolate hearts and dip them into white melted couverture chocolate?

back to basics   basic tool kit p. 9 ... tempering p. 11 ... lollipops pp. 28–29 ...

suppliers

UK

Tracey's Cakes Ltd
5 Wheelwright Road
Longwick
Bucks
HP27 9ST
Tel: 01844 347147
www.traceyscakes.co.uk
*Manufacturer of chocolate paste,
supplier of transfer sheets and
chocolate cigarillos*

Club Green
The Tyrell Building
Long Reach
Ockham
Woking
Surrey
GU23 6PG
Tel: 01483 281313
www.clubgreen.com
*For ribbons, packaging and crystal
decorations*

Dummies Direct
105 Lakey Lane
Hall Green
Birmingham
B28 9DT
01217 784692
www.dummiesdirect.co.uk
For polystyrene cake dummies

Edable Art
Furness Close
Poynton
Cheshire
SK12 1QN
Tel: 01625 878540
For dusting colours and glitters

FPC Sugarcraft
Hill View
Parfitts Hill
St George
Bristol
BS5 8BN
Tel: 01179 853249
www.fpcsc.co.uk
For rubber moulds

Home Chocolate Factory
Unit 1750
SafeStore
1,000 North Circular Road
London
NW2 7JP
Tel: 020 8450 1523
Email: enquiries@
homechocolatefactory.com
www.homechocolatefactory.com
Supplier of moulds for chocolate

Keylink Limited
Green Lane
Ecclesfield
Sheffield
S35 9WY
Tel: 01142 455400,
www.keylink.org
*Suppliers of chocolate,
fillings, décor, equipment and
packaging for the chocolatier
and patisserie industry*

Lindy's Cakes Ltd
Unit 2, Station Approach
Wendover, Aylsebury
Bucks
HP22 6BN
Tel: 01296 623906
www.lindyscakes.co.uk
For butterfly stencil and cutters

Orchard Products
Tel: 0800 9158 226
www.orchardproducts.co.uk
*For decorating tools and
food colours*

Patchwork Cutters
123 Saughall Massie Road
Wirral
Merseyside
CH49 4LA
Tel: 01516 78 5053
www.patchworkcutters.co.uk
For decorating cutters/embossers

A Piece of Cake
18–20 Upper High Street
Thame
Oxon
OX9 3EX
Tel: 01844 213428
www.apieceofcakethame.co.uk
*Sugarcraft retailer and stockist of
the gerbera cutter*

Squires Kitchen
Squires House
3 Waverley Lane
Farnham
Surrey
GU9 8BB
0845 22 55 671
www.squires-group.co.uk
For mini heart shape tins

US

Chocolate Man
16580 35th Ave NE
Lake Forest Park
WA 98155-6606
Tel: 206 365 2025
Email: orders@chocolateman.com
www.chocolateman.com
*For moulds, foils and transfer
sheets*

Green River Chocolates
961B US Route 2
Middlesex
VT 05602
Tel: 802 229 2090
www.grchocolates.com
*For domestic, imported, organic
and fair trade chocolate*

Vintage Plantations Chocolates
The University of Chocolate
461 Frelinghuysen Avenue
Newark
NJ 07114
Tel: 908 354 9304,
1 800 207 7058
Fax: 973 242 1998
Email: information@echocolates.com
www.echocolates.com
*For couverture chocolate and
cocoa butter*

Wilton Industries Inc.
2240 West 75th Street
Woodridge
1l 60517
Tel: + 1 800 794 5866
www.wilton.com
Supplier of professional bakeware

Abbreviations used in this book:

cg	Club Green
ea	Edable Art
fpc	FPC Sugarcraft
lc	Lindy's Cakes Ltd
hc	Home Chocolate Factory
k	Keylink Limited
op	Orchard Products
sk	Squires Kitchen
tc	Tracey's Cakes
pc	Patchwork Cutters
poc	A Piece of Cake
w	Wilton

acknowledgments

I am eternally grateful to my mother, Susan – the buttercream novelty cakes that she made for me as a child have inspired a career in sugarcraft and chocolate, a job that I love. I would like to thank my husband Chris, for his unending support, patience(!) and sense of humour; my 'Longwick Friends' for their part in keeping me relatively sane; Erica Galvin, a fantastic cake decorator and friend who has the most wonderful stories; Ann Gower, who taught me at the beginning; and Jennifer Fox-Proverbs for asking me to write this book – a lifelong ambition has been achieved.

about the author

Tracey Mann owns a highly successful cake design business, Tracey's Cakes. She also teaches classes in chocolate work, full details of which can be found at www.traceyscakes.co.uk. Her designs are regularly featured in *Cake* magazine and *Wedding Cakes – A Design Source* magazine. Her online mail order company now produces its own brand of chocolate paste and sells transfer sheets, chocolate and cigarillos.

index